My Amazing Story Book

INSTRUCTIONS

Enjoy the fun facts about each of the animals. You can also use these facts to inspire you in your short story.

You can color the images and leave as is.
You can color the images and add to the scenes as you wish – get creative and have some fun!

Use your imagination or a real-life event to create a short story to complete the scene.
Don't forget to give your story a title!

This story book belongs to:

____

Fun facts about...

BEARS

1. Bears can run up to 40 miles per hour.

2. Bears hibernate (a dormant state) for about 100 days in the winter.

3. Bears walk flat footed like humans do rather than on their toes like most animals. This allows them to walk upright like people.

Title:

Story:

Fun facts about...

CAMELS

1. Some camels have one hump, and some have two.

2. A camel's hump is filled with fat not water.

3. Camels have two sets of eyelashes to protect their eyes from sand.

Title:

Story:

Fun facts about...

CATS

1. A cat can jump up to eight feet in the air.

2. On average, a cat usually sleeps about 13 hours a day.

3. Cats hear better than both dogs and humans and can turn their ears 180 degrees.

Title:

Story:

____

____

____

____

____

____

____

____

Fun facts about...

COWS

1. A cow's stomach has four parts.

2. A dairy cow can produce up to 400 glasses of milk a day.

3. A cow has 32 teeth; which is, the same number as a human.

Title:

Story:

Fun facts about...

CROWS

1. Crows are known for their problem- solving skills and amazing communication skills.

2. Crows can be a symbol of luck according to the Bible.

3. Crow can mimic human speech.

Title:

Story:

____

____

____

____

____

____

____

____

____

Fun facts about...

DEER

1.   Deer can jump as high as ten feet and as far as 30 feet.

2.   Male deer grow new antlers each year.

3.   Most deer are born with white spots but lose them within a year.

Title:

Story:
____
____
____
____
____
____
____
____

Fun facts about...

DOGS

1. A dog's sense of smell is 40 times greater than human.

2. Dogs can sniff and breathe at the same time.

3. Dogs sweat from their paws and nose.

Title:

Story:

____

____

____

____

____

____

____

____

Fun facts about...

DONKEYS

1. A donkey can remember things that happened 25 years ago.

2. If a donkey feels fear, it will dig in their heels and not move.

3. Donkeys curl up their top lip and expose their front teeth when they find a new smell.

Title:

Story:

Fun facts about...

DUCKS

1. Ducks love to surf! They have been observed riding the waves of the ocean to shore and swimming back out again to do it all over.

2. Ducks are found everywhere in the world except Antarctica which is too cold for them.

3. Ducks have webbed feet and waterproof feathers that make them excellent swimmers.

Title:

Story:

Fun facts about...

ELEPHANTS

1. Human babies use a pacifier or thumb-sucking for comfort. Baby elephants suck their own trunks for comfort.

2. An elephant can not jump.

3. Elephants spend 16 hours a day eating and can live to be 70.

Title:

Story:

____

____

____

____

____

____

____

____

Fun facts about...
FROGS

1. A group of frogs is called an army.

2. Frogs don't drink water. Instead, they absorb water directly through their skin.

3. Frogs can jump over 20 times their own body length.

Title:

Fun facts about...

GIRAFFES

1. A male giraffe can grow up to 18 feet, while a female giraffe can grow up to 14 feet

2. The legs of a giraffe average about six feet and their tails can be up to 8 feet long.

3. No two giraffes have the same set of spots. Even the giraffes are telling us that being unique is awesome!

Title:

Story:

____

____

____

____

____

____

____

____

Fun facts about...

GORILLAS

1. Gorillas have hands and feet like humans including opposable thumbs and big toes.

2. Some gorillas in captivity have learned to use sign language to communicate with humans.

3. Gorillas live in small groups called troops or bands and sleep at night in nests.

Title:

Story:

Fun facts about...

HEDGEHOGS

1. They are naturally immune to snake venom and they roll into a ball to protect themselves from danger.

2. They root through "hedges" seeking their prey — mostly insects, as well as worms, centipedes, bird eggs, snails, mice, frogs, and snakes — while emitting snorts, squeals, and grunts with their "pig-like" snouts.

3. A hedgehog has between 5,000 and 7,000 quills.

Title:

Story:

____

____

____

____

____

____

____

____

Fun facts about...

HENS

1. Chickens (hens) can distinguish between more than 100 faces of their own species.

2. Chickens (hens) know who's boss—they form complex social structures known as "pecking orders," and every chicken knows his or her place on the social ladder.

3. Chickens (hens) are real sleeping beauties—they experience rapid eye movement (REM) sleep, which means they dream just like we do.

Title:

Story:

Fun facts about...
HORSES

1. A typical horse needs between 2.5 – 3 hours of sleep a day and they can sleep standing up and lying down.

2. Horses have lived on Earth for more than 50 million years and originated in North American.

3. A baby horse is called a foal. A female horse is called a mare. A male horse is called a stallion.

Title:

Story:

____

____

____

____

____

____

____

____

Fun facts about...
KANGAROOS

1. Most kangaroos are left-handed.

2. Kangaroos are mammals, and they are also marsupials. A marsupial is an animal that carries their young around in a pouch. Baby kangaroos are called joeys.

3. Kangaroos can hop around quickly on two legs or walk around slowly on all four, but they can't walk backwards.

Title:

Story:

Fun facts about...
KOALAS

1. Koalas aren't bears – they're marsupials!

2. 'Koala' is thought to mean 'no drink' in the Australian Aboriginal language. It was thought that koalas didn't need to drink because of the moisture they get from munching on juicy eucalyptus leaves all day. However, they do drink from various water sources when needed, especially during heatwaves and in times of drought.

3. Koalas can sleep up to 18 hours a day.

Title:

Story:

____

____

____

____

____

____

____

____

Fun facts about...

LIONS

1. Lions are the only cats that live in groups. A group, or pride, can be up to 30 lions, depending on how much food and water is available.

2. Female lions are the main hunters. A lion's roar can be heard up to eight kilometers or 5 miles away.

3. Lions scent mark their territory, using their wee, to create a border.

Title:

Story:

Fun facts about...
MICE

1. A mouse or plural mice is a small mammal from the rodent order of animals and are usually nocturnal animals.

2. Mice tails can grow as long as their bodies.

3. In 1928, Walt Disney's Micky Mouse was the first mouse character to be used in children cartoons and animation. Mouse characters have remained popular since with other such as Speedy Gonzales, Jerry from Tom and Jerry, and Stuart Little.

Title:

Story:

____

____

____

____

____

____

____

____

Fun facts about...

MONKEYS

1. Groups of monkeys are known as a 'tribe', 'troop' or 'mission'.

2. Monkeys are highly intelligent animals and the first monkey in space was called named Albert.

3. Monkeys can hold and grasp things with both their fingers and toes and they are known for peeling their bananas and tossing the skins aside.

Title:

Story:

Fun facts about...
OWLS

1. Owls can't move their eyes. They must turn their heads to see and can turn their heads almost completely around.

2. There are around 200 different owl species and a group of owls is called a parliament.

3. Owls cannot actually chew their food because they do not have teeth. They use their beak to tear apart their food and eat it.

Title:

Story:
____
____
____
____
____
____
____
____
____

Fun facts about...

PARROTS

1. Winston Churchill and King Henry VIII kept parrots as pets.

2. Parrots eat fruit, nuts, seeds, buds, flowers and even insects and can live up to 80 years old.

3. Parrots have a special talent — they can imitate human speech. They're not talking to communicate, but they can say words and even sing.

Title:

Story:

Fun facts about...
PENGUINS

1. Penguins are birds that cannot fly and a group of penguins in the water is called a raft but on land they're called a waddle!

2. Each penguin has a unique call.

3. No penguins live at the North Pole. Most penguins live in the Southern Hemisphere; however, large penguin populations can be found in countries such as New Zealand, Australia, Chile, Argentina and South Africa.

Title:

Story:

____

____

____

____

____

____

____

Fun facts about...

PIGS

1. Pigs are some of the cleanest animals around and refuse to defecate where they sleep and eat if given the choice. Even newborn piglets will leave their sleeping areas to relieve themselves!

2. Pigs have the intelligence of a human toddler and are ranked as the fifth most intelligent animal in the world and are more intelligent and trainable than any breed of dog.

3. Mother pigs sing to their babies and love belly rubs!

Title:

Story:

____

____

____

____

____

____

____

____

Fun facts about...
RABBITS

1. Happy rabbits practice a cute behavior known as a "binky:" they jump up in the air and twist and spin around.

2. Did you know that more than half of the world's population of rabbits actually live in North America?

3. Rabbits teeth are always growing.

Title:

Story:

____

____

____

____

____

____

____

____

Fun facts about...

SHEEP

1. Female sheep are called ewes, male sheep are called rams, and the process of giving birth is called lambing. A group of sheep is called a flock. Within only minutes, newly born lambs can stand and are walking with the flock almost immediately.

2. Sheep have an excellent sense of smell and even have scent glands in front of their eyes and on their feet.

3. Sheep have rectangular pupils which allow them to have a 270 to 320 degree field of vision. This means that they can see almost everything around them, except for what's directly behind them, without having to turn their heads.

Title:

Story:

____
____
____
____
____
____
____
____

Fun facts about...
SQUIRRELS

1. Squirrels are responsible for planting thousands of trees worldwide, due to simply forgetting where they buried their acorns.

2. Baby squirrels are called kits or kittens. They are born blind and spend their first few weeks in a nest or a den, depending on the species.

3. A squirrel that flicks its tail in snappy, arced movements is likely frustrated and showing a reactionary emotion akin to someone stomping their foot in frustration.

Title:

Story:

____

____

____

____

____

____

____

____

Fun facts about...
SWANS

1. Swans are the largest animals in the duck-goose family and have about 25,000 feathers on its body.

2. Swans can sleep on either land or the water. They have the option of sleeping while standing on one leg or while floating in the water.

3. Swans mate for life and each mate is protective of the other. Swans even touch beaks to kiss. When they kiss, their necks form a heart.

Title:

Story:

Fun facts about...

TIGERS

1. Tigers love to swim and play in the water.

2. Tigers can reach a length of up to 11 feet and weigh as much as 720 pounds. That's heavier than a piano.

3. A group of tigers is known as an 'ambush' or 'streak'. Tigers have been known to reach speeds up to 40 miles per hour.

Title:

Story:

____

____

____

____

____

____

____

____

Fun facts about...

____

Title:

Story:
____

____

____

____

____

____

____

Fun facts about...

____

Title:

Story:

Be sure and check out our
Kindle Version of this book!